UNIVERSITY *of* CAMBRIDGE
ESOL Examinations

Top Tips for IELTS
General Training

Produced by Cambridge ESOL
in collaboration with the British Council

Acknowledgements

Cambridge ESOL is grateful to the following authors and publishers for permission to reproduce copyright material in the text:

The Association of Train Operating Companies for the text on page 44, adapted from National Rail Family Railcard leaflet © Family and Friends Rail Card and The Association of Train Operating Companies; Footprint Handbooks for the adapted text on page 45 from the Footprint Australia Handbook © Footprint Handbooks; BBC Focus Magazine for the adapted text on page 46 © British Broadcasting Corporation; The Guardian for the text on page 48, adapted from 'Working from home' from Guardian Work, 25 April 2009 © Guardian News & Media; The Guardian for the text on page 55, adapted from 'Mars' from Guardian G2, 27 January 2009 © Guardian News & Media.

Every effort has been made to identify the copyright owners of material used, but it has not always been possible to identify the source or contact the copyright holders. In such cases, Cambridge ESOL would welcome information from the copyright owners.

Cambridge ESOL would also like to thank the following for their contributions to this project:

Margaret Matthews, Felicity O'Dell, Lucy Gubbin and Carole Allsop.

Illustrations by Sandra Lockwood, Artworks Design.

University of Cambridge ESOL Examinations
1 Hills Road, Cambridge, CB1 2EU, UK
www.CambridgeESOL.org

© UCLES 2009

First published 2009
Reprinted 2013

Printed in the United Kingdom by Latimer Trend

ISBN: 978-1-906438-73-9

Contents

Introduction

Top Tips for IELTS is an essential part of your revision for the International English Language Testing System (IELTS) test.

Each of the four main sections (Listening, Reading, Writing and Speaking) follows the same structure and is based on a series of pieces of advice (the 'tips') which IELTS' materials writers have collected from many years' experience of involvement in the production of IELTS tests. Each section starts with a tip at the top of the page. The tip is followed by an example taken from IELTS material and a clear explanation to help you understand exactly what it means. Each section ends with some more 'General tips' for that component.

There is also a handy section at the beginning of the book on how to revise for IELTS and a very important section at the back on what you should do on the day of the test.

There is a companion publication to this book, *Top Tips for IELTS Academic*. Please note that the Listening and Speaking sections are common to both books.

IELTS is jointly managed by British Council, University of Cambridge ESOL Examinations (Cambridge ESOL) and IDP: IELTS Australia.

How to use *Top Tips for IELTS*

Take the *Top Tips for IELTS* book with you and read it when you have a few minutes during the day. Then use the CD-ROM to practise at home: it contains an IELTS practice test for you to try, together with the answers for Listening and Reading and some sample answers for the Writing. The CD-ROM also includes all the recordings for the Listening and a video of a candidate doing an example IELTS Speaking test, to show you exactly what you will have to do when you take the test. Practise with some classmates using the Speaking test material on the CD-ROM and compare your performance with the student on the video.

Top Tips for IELTS is flexible. You can look at a different tip from a different section every day, or you can start at the beginning with the tips for the Listening test and work through until you get to the end of the tips for the Speaking test. Whichever method you prefer, read the example and the explanation carefully to make sure that you understand each tip. When you have understood all the tips for each section, try the test on the CD-ROM.

Guide to symbols

This symbol introduces the 'tip' which is at the top of the page. Each tip is some useful advice to help you find the right answer for Listening and Reading. For Writing, the tips show you how to write a better answer to the question, and for Speaking, they explain how you can give good answers which show your true level of English to the examiner.

This is an extra piece of advice which is important for this particular part of the test.

This symbol tells you to go to the CD-ROM, where you will find an IELTS practice test to try.

We hope that *Top Tips for IELTS* will help you with your preparation for taking the IELTS test.

Cambridge ESOL

Guide to question types used in IELTS Reading and Listening

Multiple choice *(Listening and Reading)* You have to read a text or listen to a recording and answer some questions. In Listening multiple-choice tasks, you usually have to choose one of three possible answers (A, B or C) for each question; in Reading you usually choose one of four (A, B, C or D). In some multiple-choice tasks, you have to choose several options from a longer list.

Identifying information *(Reading)* You have to read a text and a series of statements and decide if the statement agrees with the information in the text ('true'), if the statement contradicts the information in the text ('false') or whether there is no information in the text to support the statement ('not given').

Identifying writer's views/claims *(Reading)* You read a text and a series of statements and say whether each statement agrees with the views/claims of the writer. For each statement, you answer 'yes' if the statement does, 'no' if the statement doesn't, or 'not given' if there is no view/claim in the text to support the statement.

Matching information *(Reading)* You have to locate specific information in a paragraph or section of a text.

Matching headings *(Reading)* You have to choose the correct headings for the paragraphs or sections of the text.

Matching features *(Reading)* You have to match numbered items to a set of features (e.g. people or dates) from the text.

Matching sentence endings *(Reading)* You are given the first half of a sentence based on a text and you choose the best way to complete it from a list of possible options.

Sentence, Summary, Note, Table, Flow-chart completion
(Listening and Reading) You listen to a recording, or read a text, and fill in the missing information. Sometimes you complete the task by choosing words from a box rather than words in a Listening/Reading text. There is a limit to the number of words you can use, so pay careful attention to this when you are deciding what your answer should be.

Form completion *(Listening)* You listen to a recording and fill in the missing information in a form. You must pay careful attention to the maximum number of words you can write for each answer.

Diagram label completion *(Reading)* You complete labels on a diagram which relate to a description contained in the text. You must pay careful attention to the maximum number of words you can write for each answer.

Short-answer questions *(Listening and Reading)* You listen to a recording, or read a text, and write short answers to questions. You must pay careful attention to the maximum number of words you can write for each answer.

Matching *(Listening)* You listen to a recording and match each numbered item to one of a list of options (A, B, C etc.) according to the information you hear.

Plan, Map, Diagram labelling *(Listening)* You listen to a recording and label the plan, map or diagram according to the information you hear.

How to revise for IELTS

It is important to use the time you have to revise for IELTS effectively. Here are some general ideas to help you do this.

Make a plan

It is a good idea to make a plan for your last month's study before the test. Think about:

- what you need to do
- how much time you have
- how you can fit what you need to do into that time.

Try to be realistic when you make your plan. If you plan to do too much, then you may soon be disappointed when you fall behind.

Think about what you need to know

Most things that you do in English will help you to improve your language skills – reading an article or watching certain TV programmes may be as useful as doing a grammar exercise.

It is very important, however, that you know exactly what you will have to do in the test. Doing some practice tests will help you develop good exam techniques and this will help you a great deal in the exam room. But don't spend all your revision time doing practice papers.

Think about what you need to improve. If you are attending an IELTS preparation course, ask your English teacher what you need to work on – listening, reading, writing, or speaking, or how English is used.

Look back at your homework. What mistakes did you make? Do you understand where you went wrong? How can you improve?

Have what you need to hand

In order to prepare for IELTS you probably need:

- a good learners' dictionary (one with examples of how words are actually used in English)
- some practice tests
- an IELTS preparation coursebook
- a good grammar book
- a vocabulary notebook
- notes or other materials from your English course (if you are doing one)
- a bilingual dictionary.

If you have access to the internet you can get some of these online – the dictionaries and samples of IELTS test materials, for instance. (See www.ielts.org and www.CambridgeESOL.org)

Also have a good supply of stationery such as pens, pencils, highlighters and paper. Some students find it convenient to write things like vocabulary on cards, which they then carry with them and look at when they have a spare moment on the bus or in a café.

Think about when and where you study

Most people find it best to study at regular times at a desk with a good light and everything they need beside them.

Some people find they work best in the early mornings, while others prefer the evenings. If possible, do most of your revision at the time of day which is best for you.

You may also find that there are other good times and places for you to study. Perhaps you could listen to some English on an mp3 player while you are doing other things. Or you could read something on your way to work or college.

Organise your revision time well

Allow time for breaks when you are revising – many students like to study for an hour and a half, for example, and then have a break for half an hour.

Vary what you do – sometimes focus on listening, sometimes on vocabulary, sometimes on writing. This will make sure that you don't neglect any aspect of the language and will also make your study more interesting.

It is sensible to do something completely different before you go to bed – go for a walk, read a relaxing book or watch a favourite film.

Enjoy your study

Find some enjoyable activities that help your English – listening to songs in English or watching a TV programme or DVD will generally help your listening and pronunciation and may also extend your vocabulary.

What do you like doing in your free time? Could you combine that with English practice? For example, if you like a particular sport or singer, or if you are interested in news or computer games, you will be able to find something in English about your interest on the internet.

Study with a friend – you can practise talking to each other in English and can perhaps help each other with any questions you have.

Keep fit

Don't forget that feeling fit and healthy will help you get good marks too:

- make sure you get enough sleep
- remember to eat well
- take some exercise.

Now here are some ideas to help you organise your revision for the individual parts of IELTS.

The IELTS Listening test

Even if you are a long way from an English-speaking country, there are a lot of things you can do these days to give you practice in the kinds of listening you will have to deal with in the IELTS Listening test. Here are some ideas:

- Go to the websites of universities in English-speaking countries – these often have links where you can listen to students or staff talking about the experience of studying in their institution.
- You can find TV and radio programmes on topics relevant to IELTS on the websites of national public broadcasting organisations like the BBC (www.bbc.co.uk.iplayer), PBS (www.pbs.org) and the Australian Broadcasting Corporation (www.abc.net). You can access some of these wherever you are in the world, but some programmes are only available to people living in the country where the broadcaster is based.
- Find the tourist information website for a country that you would like to visit – such websites often now have video clips which provide useful listening materials.
- Many libraries and museums now also have websites with video materials which can provide useful listening practice.
- Search YouTube (www.youtube.com) for interesting recordings – use keywords like 'lecture' or 'tutorial', or 'study skills' and you should find plenty of clips to help you practise.

The IELTS General Training Reading test

The more you read before the test, the better you will do. Reading is also a very good way of improving your vocabulary and grammar and it will also help your own writing.

The General Training Reading test includes a wide range of texts including such practically useful texts as notices, advertisements, timetables, information about travel and accommodation, company handbooks and contracts as well as articles from newspapers, magazines or journals and extracts from fiction and non-fiction books.

- Make sure you read from a wide range of sources including something from each of the text types listed above – you can easily find examples of all of these on the internet as well as in printed form.

- It's important to read for pleasure, so regularly read something that you enjoy – novels, sports reports or magazine quizzes may not feature in IELTS but reading them will also help you develop your knowledge of the language in an effective way.
- Keep a reading diary – write a couple of sentences in English about what you have read. This should also help you to learn some of the words and expressions you have read and will also help you with the IELTS Writing test.
- Discuss what you have read with a friend – perhaps start a reading club to do this on a regular basis.
- Don't look up every word that you are not sure about when you read. Just look up anything that seems to be important for a general understanding of the text. When you have finished reading you can then, if you want, go back and check the meanings of less important vocabulary.

Other examples of things you might like to read include:
- graded readers and magazines
- translations of books you have already read in your own language
- travel information about your own country or places you have been to
- newspaper articles
- music, film or book reviews.

The IELTS General Training Writing test

The General Training Writing test asks you to write a letter and an essay giving your opinion on a topic.

- Practise writing answers to exam type tasks on a regular basis – if possible, ask a teacher or other good English speaker to correct your work. Pay attention to the comments they make and try to improve in the next piece of writing you do for them.
- Always think about the structure of what you are going to write – make a plan first.
- Always think about who the task says you are writing for – how does this affect what you need to write and how you should express it?
- In your writing make a point of using new words and expressions that you have recently learned – if necessary use a good learner's dictionary for good examples of how words are used in practice.

- Practise checking your writing carefully so that it is as accurate as possible – look particularly for the kinds of mistakes that you know you often make (mistakes with verb agreement, prepositions or articles, for example).
- Make sure that you know the conventions in English for writing different kinds of letters.

The IELTS Speaking test

Make the effort to practise speaking in English whenever you can.

- Make sure that you know how to talk about your own work and study experiences and plans – become familiar with the relevant language by reading articles on the internet about, for example, your chosen profession and about university courses.
- Make sure that you know how to express your opinion on a range of general topics, giving examples and reasons to explain why you think as you do – become familiar with the relevant language by listening to radio or watching TV programmes in which people give their opinions.
- If there are students in your area whose first language is English, try to make contact with them – perhaps you could exchange conversation sessions with them – half an hour in English and half an hour in your first language.
- Try to make contact with English-speaking visitors to your area – perhaps you could get some part-time work as a tour guide.
- Practise with friends by agreeing to only talk English for half an hour on a regular basis – choose a specific topic to discuss for that time.
- Join an English language club if there is one in your area.
- Make sure that you can do these things with ease in English – introduce yourself, agree or disagree, ask someone to repeat or explain, give arguments for and against, make hypotheses, talk about your own experiences, justify a point of view – as you will almost certainly need to do most of these in the exam.

We hope these ideas will help you to make the most of your revision time. Above all, we hope that you enjoy your studies and wish you all the best for your exam.

The IELTS Listening test

What's in the Listening test?

Section 1 @ a conversation in an everyday social context between two people

Section 2 @ a monologue on a topic relating to general social needs

Section 3 @ a conversation in an academic context between two or more people

Section 4 @ a lecture or talk on a topic of general academic interest

☑ 1 mark for each correct answer

 Approximately **40 minutes**
(including 10 minutes to copy your answers onto the answer sheet)

Each section has 10 questions.

The following question types are used in the Listening test:

- multiple choice
- matching
- plan, map, diagram labelling
- note completion
- form completion

- table completion
- sentence completion
- short answer questions
- summary completion
- flow-chart completion

Any of these question types may appear in any section. Not all question types will appear in an individual Listening test.

Listening: multiple choice

 TIP: Don't choose an option just because you hear a word from it. Think about the whole meaning of what is said.

Example

Here is a question from a task about a field trip.

> **What did the students see on their walk in the mountains?**
>
> A a group of unusual animals
>
> B some rare plants ✓
>
> C an interesting geological feature

TAPESCRIPT

TUTOR:	How did you enjoy the field trip to Scotland?
STUDENT:	Well, we had some fantastic walks. One day we walked along an amazing deserted beach. We must have walked for about fifteen miles and we saw a seal which was basking in the sunshine. It was there all by itself.
TUTOR:	How lucky! They're such beautiful animals and it's quite unusual to see them there.
STUDENT:	That's right. Another day we climbed the mountain behind the hut where we were staying. We were hoping to find some rare ferns that are supposed to grow there and nowhere else in Scotland. We'd just about given up hope when we found some at the bottom of a rocky slope. They have a number of very interesting features, for example ...

Explanation: The correct answer is B, but the mention of an unusual animal (a seal, although only one) might lead you to believe that A is correct. Similarly, the phrase 'interesting features' might tempt you to the answer C. In other words, you need to understand the recording as a whole rather than jump to a conclusion simply because you hear words from one of the options.

Listening: multiple choice

 TIP: Sometimes in a multiple-choice question you have to complete a half sentence with one of the options. If you change the first half sentence into a question it often makes it easier to choose the right answer.

Example

Here is a question from a task about a lecture on a scientific experiment.

 The study was carried out in order to

A determine the health benefits of eating tomatoes.

B investigate whether tomato tablets could protect against heart disease. ✓

C establish the side-effects of a range of nutritional supplements.

 As we are all well aware, some nutritional supplements have some undesirable side-effects. The Robinson research that we're going to look at today seems to have determined quite conclusively that the tomato tablets under consideration have no significant side-effects at all. However, his main focus was on their health benefits. It's long been known that a diet rich in tomatoes seems to be very good for our hearts. However, until recently it has been impossible to preserve the health-giving, antioxidant properties of tomatoes in tablet form. Robinson wanted to find out whether these supplements would really have the same health benefits as a tomato-rich diet.

TAPESCRIPT

Explanation: In this case the question would be 'Why was the study carried out?' and the correct answer is **B**. **A** is incorrect because the speaker says that the health benefits of eating tomatoes have long been known – there was therefore no need for a further study into this. **C** is incorrect because it relates only to the side-effects of tomato tablets (and not a range of nutritional supplements) and also because the issue of side-effects was not the main focus of the study.

Listening: multiple choice

 TIP: You will hear some reference to all the options in the list, but some of them will not be an appropriate answer to the question.

Example

Here is a question from a task relating to a student's lab report.

 Which two sections of her work does the student need to improve?

A conclusion ✓

B figures ✓

C procedure

D results

E aims

TAPESCRIPT

STUDENT: How was my lab report this time? Do you think it was better than my last one?

TUTOR: Yes, it was much improved, particularly the clear way in which you described the procedure. I also felt you laid out the aims very clearly, which gave a good impression from the start. You could think a bit more in future about the conclusions section, though. That felt a bit hurried to me even though you'd actually made a first-class job of writing up the results.

STUDENT: What about the way I presented the figures? Was that OK?

TUTOR: Yes, I liked it. But don't forget that you need to label them all and then you can refer to them more easily when you're describing them in your text.

Explanation: The tutor suggests that the student can improve the conclusion **A** and the figures **B**.

The tutor makes positive comments about procedure **C**, results **D** and aims **E**.

Listen to everything the speaker says before you choose the answer, in order to be sure that you are selecting the correct options.

Listening: multiple choice

 TIP: You may find it useful to cross out each option that you hear being eliminated.

Example

Here is a question from a task relating to a lecture on languages.

> **Q** **Which three things is the lecture course going to cover?**
> **A** ~~grammar~~
> **B** language change ✓
> **C** language families
> **D** multilingualism ✓
> **E** ~~pronunciation~~
> **F** sociolinguistics ✓
> **G** ~~vocabulary~~

TAPESCRIPT

Welcome to the first lecture in our course on linguistics. **F**
Today I'm going to start off with a brief look at the
relationship between society and language and we'll continue
with that topic next week. However, first I'm going to give
you just a quick overview of what the course will cover over
and above that first topic. So, last year we looked together
at aspects of language such as vocabulary and how words
combine to communicate meaning in a way that is considered
'grammatically correct' by the language's speakers. We're
leaving these aspects of language now to take a slightly
broader view. We'll look for instance at how people cope in **D**
societies where it's necessary for them to operate in more
than one language. This is the case for a surprisingly large
number of people who speak one language in their family and
another at school or work. I'll leave for the moment issues
relating to pronunciation as you'll be having a separate
phonology course from Dr Thompson in the next semester.
However, how languages have developed over time will be the **B**
third important theme of this course.

Explanation: The correct answers are **B**, **D** and **F**. Both grammar **A** and vocabulary **G** were dealt with last year. Pronunciation **E** will be covered on a different course. The speaker doesn't refer to language families **C** – his use of the word family is in relation to bilingualism.

The options don't follow the order in which you hear them on the recording. So make sure that you read them all first and keep them all in mind as you answer the questions.

Listening: matching

 TIP: The numbered items appear in the order in which you hear them, but the options (A–F) do not. Make sure that you read all the options before the recording starts.

Example

Here are two items from a task about finding temporary work.

 What does Jenny say about each type of job?

Jenny's opinion

A good opportunity to gain useful experience

B hours tend to be inconvenient

C jobs available for people with specific skills

D pay is surprisingly good

E plenty of work at the moment

F work is popular with students

Jobs

1 hotel work ....**D**....

2 telephone sales ....**F**....

TAPESCRIPT

There are plenty of opportunities for temporary work in hotels available at the moment. It's quite hard work but you don't need any special skills. You can actually earn a lot more than you might imagine and it's often possible to choose the hours that are most convenient for you.

You might also be interested in doing something in telesales. It doesn't matter if you haven't got any previous experience of this. It's work which local undergraduates often choose to do. The hours tend to fit in well with lectures and other university commitments.

Explanation: 'You can earn a lot more than you might imagine' is another way of saying the 'pay is surprisingly good' **D**. The last two sentences make it clear, using quite different words, that the 'work is popular with students' **F**.

The words that you hear that give you the right answer may not be the same as the words on the page. On the other hand, you may hear the exact word from one of the options, but this does not necessarily mean that it is the right answer.

Listening: map labelling

 TIP: Listen carefully for the starting point – you need to start at the correct place in order to get the questions right.

Example

Here is the start of a task about a shopping mall.

Q **Label the map below.**

Waterside Shopping Mall

North entrance

A

Sporty Sports

West entrance

East entrance

B

Freshfields Supermarket

Brian's Music

C

Jones department store

South entrance

Toni's Shoes

Car park

You are here

1 pizza restaurant . . . . **B** . . . .

TAPESCRIPT

OK, we're at the south entrance to the mall now. I'll tell you where some of the main shops are and then you can go off and explore on your own. Can we meet up though at the pizza restaurant at half past twelve? You'll find that about halfway along this street in front of us now. If you come to the fountain, that means you've gone too far. It's just before that on the left-hand side.

Explanation: It's very important to locate yourself in the right place. For example, if you start at the west rather than the south entrance then you will think the pizza restaurant is at **A** rather than **B**.

Listening: map labelling

 TIP: Use the pause before you listen to think about the words the speaker might use to describe the map or diagram.

Example

This example comes from a task relating to a motor show.

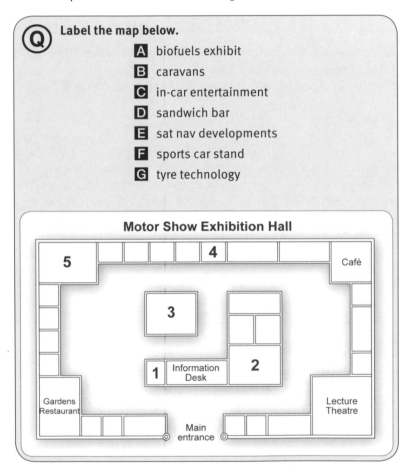

Label the map below.

A biofuels exhibit

B caravans

C in-car entertainment

D sandwich bar

E sat nav developments

F sports car stand

G tyre technology

Motor Show Exhibition Hall

5

4

Café

3

1 Information Desk

2

Gardens Restaurant

Lecture Theatre

Main entrance

1 .... **C** ....

2 .... **A** ....

TAPESCRIPT

When you get to the Motor Show you'll find it's in an enormous hall and it would be quite easy to miss some of the most interesting exhibits, so I'd like to give you a bit of general information first. First of all, there is a small stand to the left of the information desk as you go into the hall. That's got a very interesting display looking at different modern technologies allowing you to listen to good quality music as you drive. Next to that, to the right of the information desk, is a very interesting area where you can see an area devoted to the development of more ecologically sound forms of petrol and diesel. I think that you will be impressed by what you see there.

C

A

Explanation: In this kind of activity you have to focus on what is in a specific place rather than on where something is. The numbers are on the map or diagram and you will hear them in the logical numerical order. It is unlikely though that the options will be referred to in exactly the same way as they are listed on the page. So you have to think in advance about how the recording might refer to the options. For example, if one of the options refers to 'biofuels' you might expect the speaker to use the words 'petrol' and 'diesel'. Similarly, when thinking about how 'in-car entertainment' could be paraphrased, you might predict the word 'music'.

Listening: matching

 TIP: Sometimes the **C** option is the **A** option plus the **B** option. Make sure that you wait to hear all the information you need before you decide on the correct answer.

Example

Here is a question from a task about facilities at a community centre and the first item from the list of facilities.

 When can the public use each of these facilities at the Community Centre?

A Weekends

B Monday to Friday

C Weekends and Monday to Friday

Facilities

1 Swimming pool . . . . **C** . . . .

 I'm pleased to say that this year Midtown Community Centre will be open to the public more than it was last year. The swimming pool has been extended and modernised and will be of great benefit to people of all ages in the town. As before, it will be open for schools every weekday during the day but everyone will be able to use it on Saturdays and Sundays from 7 in the morning until 9 at night. However, due to popular request it will now also be open for general use every evening during the week too.

TAPESCRIPT

Explanation: The first part of what the speaker says suggests that the answer is going to be **A**. However, it is important to continue listening, otherwise you will miss the information that public use is also possible from Monday to Friday in the evenings **C**.

Listening: note completion

 TIP: Listen for words that indicate the structure of the talk (words like 'first', 'next', 'finally' and so on) as these will help to guide you through the notes on the page.

Example

This is an example from a task based on a lecture about business organisations. You have to use no more than two words and/or a number.

 Complete the notes below.

Hofstede – study of 1 ... *cultural differences* ...

Analysed people in terms of:

- attitudes to change
- attitudes to **2** ... *power* ...
- masculine/feminine qualities
- individualist/**3** ... *communal* ... values

TAPESCRIPT

Having looked last week at Weber's study of bureaucracy we're now going to go on and consider Hofstede's seminal work on cultural differences. He analysed 41 different nationalities and attempted to characterise them in terms of where they lay on four separate scales. Firstly, he considered how easy or difficult they found it to deal with change. Secondly, he looked at each nationality from the point of view of how they dealt with power. The next parameter related to the extent to which they exemplified what Hofstede refers to as masculine or feminine characteristics. And finally, he looked at whether the nationality's values tended to be communal or individualist.

Explanation: It is clear that **1** must relate to a topic for a study of some kind, **2** must relate to attitudes in society, and **3** must be an adjective that contrasts with 'individualist'. Preparing yourself like this before you listen will help you choose the right answers.

Listening: form completion

 TIP: Make sure that you are totally familiar with the names of the letters in English and the sounds which often cause you confusion. This task often asks you to write down words that are spelled out.

Example

Here is a question from a task about joining a social club. You have to write the name of the person who wants to join.

 Complete the form below.

HORSHAM CLUB

MEMBERSHIP APPLICATION

Name: Jane **1** ... *Tressinghay* ...

TAPESCRIPT

MAN: OK, so you'd like to join Horsham Club. Can I first take some details? What's your full name, please?

WOMAN: It's Jane Tressinghay.
That's T-R-E-double-S-I-N-G-H-A-Y.

MAN: Tressinghay. That's an unusual name.

Explanation: Spelling questions are easy to get right if you know your alphabet in English. Practise with a friend if possible, so that it becomes easy for you. Practise dictating each other letters – and numbers too.

 *Reference numbers and postcodes often include both letters and numbers and these are often tested in form completion tasks.*

Listening: table completion

 TIP: Listen carefully – the recording may also include information that could fit in the gap but is not the correct answer.

Example

This example comes from a task about an arts festival. You have to use no more than two words and/or a number.

(Q) Complete the table below.

MARYBRIDGE ARTS FESTIVAL		
Event	**When?**	**Where?**
1 ... *poetry reading* ...	Friday, May 16th, 7 pm	**2** ... *Town Hall* ...

TAPESCRIPT

This year's Marybridge Arts Festival will be hosting a large number of popular events and I'm here to tell you about some of them tonight. The Festival opens on Friday 16th May. There'll be an opening ceremony at 6 pm and that will be followed by a poetry reading. That will start at 7 pm and will feature a number of well-known performance poets. Please note that this event will take place in the Town Hall, but most of the other festival events will be in the Kings Theatre.

Explanation: Two events are mentioned in the recording – the opening ceremony and the poetry reading. The times of these make it clear that the answer to **1** is the poetry reading. Similarly, two venues are mentioned in the recording – the Town Hall and the Kings Theatre. You need to listen carefully to choose the right one for **2** (the Town Hall).

Listening: **sentence completion**

TIP: Be careful that what you write fits grammatically with the other words in the sentence and is spelled correctly.

Example

This is part of a task in which two business students are discussing a group project. Use no more than two words and/or a number.

 Complete the sentences below.

1 This year's group project involves designing a
... *TV advert* ...

2 Meena missed the group project last year because of
... *computer problems* ...

TAPESCRIPT

TIM:	I'm quite looking forward to this term's group project. I really enjoyed last year's one.
MEENA:	Did you, Tim? I had to miss it, I'm afraid. You had to design a company logo, didn't you? A lot easier than planning a TV advert like we've got to do now.
TIM:	You're right Meena. But why didn't you take part last year? Was it because of illness?
MEENA:	Actually it was because I had computer problems and I just couldn't manage to sort them out in time!

Explanation: For **1**, if you just write 'advert' without 'TV', then it does not fit grammatically with the article 'a' and you would not get the mark. For **2**, if you just write either 'computer' or 'problems' it does not make total sense and you would not get the mark.

Remember to check your work carefully. Make sure that your grammar and spelling are correct.

Listening: short-answer questions

 TIP: You will hear the exact word or words you need. You don't have to change them in any way.

Example

Here is a question from a task about booking a holiday. Use no more than three words and/or a number.

 Answer the questions below.

1 What does the man want to do on holiday?
... *see wild animals* ...

2 What kind of accommodation would he prefer?
... *self-catering* ...

TAPESCRIPT

WOMAN: OK, I can certainly make some suggestions for you about your trip to South Africa. But, first, I need to know what kind of thing you enjoy doing on holiday.

MAN: Well, normally, my wife and I just like to relax on holiday, sunbathe, read, that sort of thing. But this is going to be a special holiday. So we want to see as much as possible, especially some wild animals.

WOMAN: Well, there are lots of opportunities to do that there! So next, can you give me an idea about the sort of accommodation you'd like while you're over there? Luxury hotel? Guesthouse? Self-catering?

MAN: Yes, that one. We do like to cook for ourselves.

Explanation: The correct answers are highlighted in the tapescript. There is no need to think of different words, for example, 'go on safari', to use in your answers.

Listening: **short-answer questions**

 TIP: Do not write more words than you are asked for – you will automatically lose marks.

Example

This is part of a task about plans for a study weekend. The instructions for this task tell you to write no more than two words.

 Answer the questions below.

1 What are the students going to study during the weekend? ... *romantic poets* ...

2 Which part of the weekend are they most looking forward to? ... *translation workshop* ...

TAPESCRIPT

MIKE:	It should be a good weekend, don't you think?
FIONA:	Yes, I do. I love the romantic poets and to have a whole weekend studying them should be great.
MIKE:	Well, it'll certainly be interesting to see how the English ones compare with other European ones, for example.
FIONA:	Yes, I just hope the English versions of poems from other languages will be good enough to give us a real impression of what the originals were like.
MIKE:	Well, the translation workshop should help us there. It focuses on how to translate poetry.
FIONA:	Mm, I'm really looking forward to that most of all.
MIKE:	Me too.

Explanation: You are asked to write no more than two words. If you write 'European romantic poets', 'the romantic poets' or 'the poetry translation workshop' you will not get the marks because you have written too many words.

Listening: summary completion

 TIP: Make sure your answers fit grammatically as well as reflecting the meaning of what you hear.

Example

This example comes from a task on the topic of product design. You should use one word only or a number in each space.

 Complete the summary below.

The QFD approach to product design is different from the so-called **1** ... *traditional* ... model in that it puts the requirements of the **2** ... *customer* ... first.

 TAPESCRIPT

Most engineers now prefer to take the QFD or quality function deployment approach to product design. This model has some significant differences in comparison with what is often referred to as the traditional approach. Of course it has to go through the same basic phases of establishing requirements, planning designs, producing and testing them. The focus, however, is that the customer and his or her needs are paramount and much more time is spent determining what exactly these are before work begins on any of the other phases.

Explanation: If you read the phrase containing the gap carefully before you listen, it will be clear that **1** needs an adjective or another word that could be used to describe a model or approach to product design. 'The' makes it clear that **2** will be a noun.

 *It's helpful to read the whole summary first before the recording starts.*

Listening: **flow-chart completion**

 TIP: You may think that you can guess the answer from your own world knowledge, but it is what the speaker says that is important and this can be different from what you might expect.

Example

Here is an example from a task about applying for a job. You have to complete the flow chart using no more than two words and/or a letter in each space.

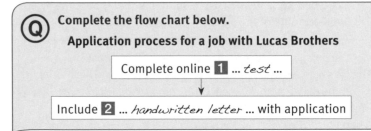

Q Complete the flow chart below.

Application process for a job with Lucas Brothers

Complete online **1** ... *test* ...

Include **2** ... *handwritten letter* ... with application

TAPESCRIPT

Now, I'd like to explain what the process is for those of you who would like to apply – or know someone who'd like to apply – for a position in one of our new offices. Of course we ask you to fill in an application form, but before doing that we'd recommend looking at our website where you'll find full details of what exactly we're looking for. That should help you to focus your application in the most appropriate way. On the site you'll also find a test which you can try to see how your profile matches what we're looking for. We ask you to do this first and there's space on our application form where you can fill in your scores. We don't require a photo or references at this point but we do also ask you to send us a handwritten letter with your application as we have also found that invaluable in our selection of new members of staff...

Explanation: From your knowledge of the world you might imagine that completing an application form is the first stage in the process of a job application, and the beginning of the recording might seem to confirm this. However, listening further it becomes clear that the answer to **1** is actually 'test'. Similarly, for **2** you might predict 'photograph' or 'references' but the correct answer is the less predictable 'handwritten letter'.

General tips for **Listening**

1 You only hear the recordings once – so write the answers as you listen.

2 Listen carefully to the introduction for each section and try to imagine what the speakers will talk about. This will give you useful information about the situation and the speakers.

3 In the real test, you have time at the beginning of each section to look at the task. Use this time well to read the questions and think about the topics.

4 The questions always follow the order of the recording. Don't panic if you miss one question – look ahead and think about the next one.

5 Write clearly when you transfer your answers to the answer sheet.

6 When you transfer your answers to the answer sheet, don't copy any extra words from the question paper.

7 When you read the question, you may find it helpful to think of words to listen for which have a similar meaning.

8 Listen to the intonation of the speaker as this could help you to decide whether the sentence is positive or negative.

9 It is useful to underline key words in the question to help you focus on the words (or similar words) to listen for.

 NOW YOU TRY! You will find a complete Listening test to try on the CD-ROM.

When you have finished you can see your scores, check and print your answers.

University of Cambridge ESOL Examinations

The IELTS Reading test

What's in the General Training Reading test?

Section 1   Two or three texts about everyday life in an English-speaking country. Each text is followed by questions which focus on specific information.

Section 2   Two texts about work-related situations. Each text is followed by questions which focus on specific information.

Section 3 Ⓠ One text that is longer than the texts in Sections 1 and 2. Questions test general, extended reading comprehension.

☑ 1 mark for each correct answer

🕐 **1 hour**

The following question types are used in the General Training Reading test:

- multiple choice
- identifying information
- identifying writer's views/claims
- matching information
- matching headings
- matching features
- matching sentence endings
- table completion
- sentence completion
- short-answer questions
- summary completion
- note completion
- flow-chart completion
- diagram label completion

Any of these question types may occur in any section. Not all question types will appear in an individual General Training Reading test.

TOP TIPS FOR **IELTS**

Reading: multiple choice

 TIP: When you have found the right place in the text, read that part carefully. Information in the text may look very similar to one of the options – but may not be the correct answer.

Example

Here is an extract from a text about meteorites, and one of the questions.

> At half past six on the morning of December 14th 1807, the folk of Weston, Connecticut, were woken by a loud bang caused by a falling meteorite. Cautiously they ventured into the streets, but were soon fleeing back to the safety of their homes as it started to rain rocks. In earlier times such hard rain might have been seen as a sign of the gods' displeasure. The folk of Weston, however, saw it as an opportunity. Strongly impressed with the idea that these stones contained gold and silver, they employed a blacksmith's anvil in a vain attempt to extract riches which only existed in their imagination.

Q **What was the reaction of the people of Weston to the meteorite?**

 A They were too scared by the noise it made to go outside.

 B They were worried it had destroyed their property.

 C They thought they had done something wrong.

 D They hoped that it might change their fortunes. ✓

40   University of Cambridge ESOL Examinations

Explanation: The highlighted words in the text show where you can find the answer. **A** is incorrect because the text says that 'they ventured into the streets' after the 'loud bang'. **B** is incorrect because the people went back to their homes to protect themselves 'fleeing back to the safety ...'. **C** is incorrect. The text says that this might have been true in earlier times, but not in 1807.

> *The last multiple-choice question in the set of questions may focus on the text in general, and test your overall understanding.*

Reading: identifying information

 TIP: Remember that the statements will not be expressed in exactly the same way as in the text.

Example

Here is an extract from a brochure on terms and conditions of booking a holiday, followed by one of the statements. You have to decide whether the statement is 'true', 'false' or 'not given'.

> Our brochure is printed long periods in advance so we must reserve the right to make alterations without notice. Certain facilities, such as the swimming pool, are available as stated but these may be withdrawn according to circumstances and demand. Please note that we do not employ lifeguards and so children and non-swimmers must be accompanied by an adult swimmer at all times. Should any guests cause problems or inconvenience to other guests, they will be asked to leave the holiday park without a refund.
>
> **1** If there are not enough people at the holiday park, the swimming pool might be closed. *TRUE*

Explanation: The highlighted words in the text show where you can find the answer. Note how the words highlighted in the text are different in the statement, but the meaning is the same.

 *Underline the key words in the statements, as this may be helpful when you are trying to locate the information in the text. (In this statement the key words are 'swimming pool' and 'closed'.)*

Reading: **identifying information**

 TIP: If the statement neither agrees with the information in the text (TRUE), nor contradicts the information in the text (FALSE), the answer is NOT GIVEN. If you are deciding whether the answer is true or false, make sure the fact is actually in the text and not just your assumption.

Example

Here is another extract from the same holiday brochure, followed by one of the statements. You have to decide whether the statement is 'true', 'false' or 'not given'.

> A limited number of dogs are allowed in the holiday park at an extra charge of £40 per week. Dogs will not be admitted into the holiday park unless advised and paid for in advance and will be strictly monitored. Dogs must be supervised and kept on a lead at all times. Proof of payment will be required and must be shown on arrival.
>
> **1** The number of dogs is restricted to one per booking.
>   *NOT GIVEN*

Explanation: The highlighted words in the text give the information about dogs at the holiday park. Although it is true that a 'limited number of dogs are allowed', the text does not say what the maximum number of dogs per booking is.

 *Do not assume you know the answer from your own general knowledge of the subject.*

Reading: matching information

 TIP: Underline the key words in the questions and then look for words with the same or opposite meanings in the text. Remember that the information in the questions will not be expressed in exactly the same words as in the text.

Example

Here are two paragraphs from a leaflet about applying for a rail card, and one of the questions.

> **A** To apply for your railcard, simply complete the application form and take it to your nearest staffed station ticket office or appointed travel agents. Station offices and agents accept cash, cheques, debit and credit cards. Postal application is not available. Please retain the leaflet receipt once it has been completed. Should you mislay your railcard and need to obtain a replacement, you will be asked to show this at the station office.
>
> **B** To renew your railcard, you will need to complete the application form and take your existing rail card with you to the station office. Remember you can renew your railcard up to one month in advance of its expiry date, providing there is no break in continuity.
>
> **Which paragraph mentions the following?**
>   **1** what to take to the station office if you lose your railcard ... **A** ...

Explanation: The highlighted part of the text shows that the answer is in Paragraph **A**. 'Lose' is a synonym for 'mislay' and 'should you' is a more formal way of saying 'if you'. (In the statement 'this' refers back to 'leaflet receipt', which is what you need to take.) Paragraph **B** is incorrect as it tells you what to take to the station office if you want to renew, rather than replace, your railcard.

Reading: matching information

 TIP: When this task appears in Section 1, there may be several short texts which have a common theme. They will contain similar information but there will be some small differences – so you will need to read the texts and questions carefully and check your answers.

Example

Here are three short extracts from a guide to restaurants in an Australian city, and one of the questions.

Dining out in Sydney

A *Takashi's* is without doubt one of the city's best restaurants. The restaurant has only recently been relocated to new and extremely stylish premises. Book well in advance and, if you can afford it, try the 12-course special dinner.

B Equally popular is *Trattoria Giovanni*, 18 Argyle Street. Set in a former warehouse, it offers fine Italian cuisine and a good wine list. Open Tues – Fri for lunch and daily for dinner.

C The Museum of Modern Design Basement Restaurant is ideally located in the harbour area. It is a bit expensive but worth it, and the seafood is excellent.

 For which restaurant is the following statement true?

1 The building in which this restaurant is situated was originally used for another purpose. . . . **B** . . . .

Explanation: **B** is correct because it states that the building was previously used as a warehouse. 'Former' has a similar meaning to 'originally used for'. **A** is incorrect because it does not say the new premises were ever used for anything else. **C** is incorrect because the building is still an art museum (with a restaurant).

Reading: matching headings

 TIP: Concentrate on the main idea of each paragraph or section by skimming and scanning for overall meaning, as this will help you find the correct heading.

Example

This is an extract from a text about space, and some of the headings.

 Choose the correct heading from the list of headings below.

> ### List of Headings
>
> i   A March launch
> ii   A new approach to space exploration
> iii The quest to find more planets ✓

A Trailing Earth on its own path around the Sun, an unmanned observatory has just begun looking for answers to a question guaranteed to have an astonishing answer: are we alone in the universe? Launched in March, NASA's Kepler probe is now settling down for three and a half years of staring unblinkingly into space, hunting for other Earths. To find them, it is scanning the light from 100,000 stars, looking for tiny dips in brightness caused by planets passing in front of them.

Explanation: The highlighted words in the text show where you can find the answer. Heading **i** is incorrect because it is focusing on one specific detail rather than the main idea of the paragraph. Heading **ii** is also incorrect because the text does not actually say that this is a new approach.

The main idea of the text is that the purpose of the mission is to look for more planets. Key words are 'looking for answers', 'hunting for other Earths'. Heading **iii** is therefore the correct heading.

Remember there will always be extra headings that you will not need to use.

Reading: matching features

 TIP: In the text it may be helpful to underline the names, dates, numbers, etc. from the questions or options, so that you can locate them quickly. One statement may match more than one item in the list.

Example

Here is an extract from a text about working from home and garden offices and one of the statements.

As working from home becomes an increasingly popular option for many workers, 'garden offices' have become big business. There are a range of sheds available for people who can no longer face the long journey to work. Some 'garden offices' retain the feel of a traditional shed-like atmosphere, such as those from the <u>Garden Room Company</u>, while with others the trend is towards eco-friendly constructions. One example of the latter is <u>Vivid Green</u>, whose main focus is low energy products. The Z model from <u>Energy Space</u> takes this one step further: the energy generated through its solar roof panels can be diverted back to the main house when you are not working in the garden office.

 Match each description with the correct company.

This company has designed a shed which can reduce existing household fuel bills.

List of Companies

A Garden Room Company
B Vivid Green
C Energy Space ✓

Explanation: The highlighted words in the text show where you can find the answer. The shed designed by Energy Space has roof panels that generate energy which can be used in the main house, and so reduce bills. Note that in the text the word 'energy' is replaced by 'fuel' in the question. 'Energy' is used in connection with Vivid Green **B** as well, but this company focuses on low energy products and eco-friendly construction. Garden Room Company **A** does not have a focus on reducing energy bills.

*The statements do not follow the order of the text but the options (**A**, **B**, **C**, etc.) do.*

Reading: table completion

 TIP: Look at the headings and key words in the table and scan the text for them. Then read that part of the text carefully.

Example

Here is an extract from a website giving information about training programmes at a supermarket chain, and one of the questions.

Betta Buys Training Programmes

Induction training is compulsory for all colleagues and takes place during your first 2 days. It is a basic introduction to our company – it explains the way we work, how to deliver great service and includes all the legal and compliance subjects such as health and safety and food safety.

Foundation training takes place during your first 12 weeks and introduces you to your role. It includes all the basics you need to know to work productively and safely in your department.

Intermediate training takes place during your first 12 months. This helps you to grow in your role and deliver to the required performance standards.

Advanced training is for management and team leader colleagues, job experts and those who want to develop for their next step. This covers how to manage and supervise.

(Q) **Complete the table below.**

Types of training programme	Timing	Content of training
Induction training	During first 2 days	Health and food safety Working methods Ways of providing good **1** ... *service* ...
Foundation training	During the first 12 weeks	
Intermediate training	During the first 12 months	
Advanced training		

Explanation: You can find the key information by scanning the text for 'induction training' and then reading that part of the text carefully.

Before you start trying to complete the gaps, make sure you look carefully at the rows and columns in the table to see how the information is organised and what you need to write where.

Reading: sentence completion

 TIP: Make sure the completed sentence is grammatically accurate and has the same meaning as the text. You will not have to change any of the words in the text, so make sure you use exactly the same ones.

Example

Here is an extract from a website giving advice about researching overseas markets, and one of the questions. In this example, your answer should be no more than two words.

Market issues

You need to understand local cultural influences in order to sell your products effectively. For example, your product may be viewed as a basic commodity at home, but not in your overseas market. Your sales and marketing approach will need to reflect this. You will also need to consider the language spoken. Can you market your product effectively in the local language? Will you have access to professional translators and marketing agencies?

 Complete the sentence below.

1 If you want people in other countries to buy your products, it is necessary to have an awareness of the ... *cultural differences* ... which there are in that area.

Explanation: The correct answer is 'cultural influences'. This is the only answer that makes sense in the sentence and is also grammatically correct. You might have thought 'language spoken' was the correct answer but although this makes sense it does not fit grammatically in the sentence. You could not change the word 'language' to 'languages' because the plural form is not in the text.

Remember to check the word limit in the instructions for each task and write no more than the number of words specified in each answer.

Reading: short-answer questions

 TIP: In this type of task the maximum number of words also varies, so check this carefully before you answer the questions.

Example

Here is part of a text about taking holiday from work, and one of the questions. In this example you have to use no more than three words from the text for each answer.

If you want to take holiday

You must give your employer advance notice that you want to take holiday. This notice should be at least twice as long as the amount of holiday you want to take (for example, you should give two weeks' notice for one week's holiday).

If your employer wants you to take holiday

Your employer can decide when some or all of your holidays must be taken. For instance, they may require you to take some of your holiday to cover national holidays, or may require the whole company to take holiday during a Christmas shutdown. This may be in your contract, or it may be normal practice built up over time. An employer has to give the same amount of notice as you do.

 Answer the question below.

1 Where can you find information about the days you have to take as holiday? ... *in your contract* ...

Explanation: The highlighted words show where you can find the answer. The answer could be 'in your contract' or 'your contract' but could not be 'may be in your contract' as this would be more than the limit of three words.

Reading: **summary completion**

TIP: Read the words surrounding the gaps in the summary carefully. Think about whether the missing word is a verb, a noun, etc. You must write the exact word as it appears.

Example

Here is part of a text about Mars and the first two sentences from the summary. You need one word for your answer.

High in the sky above Mars it is snowing. The snow does not settle on the rubble-strewn land below but instead vaporises into the thin atmosphere long before it reaches the ground. The news of falling snow is just one piece of an extraordinary wealth of information that has recently been sent back to Earth by orbiters, landers and rovers. Together they have mapped the surface in unprecedented detail, cracked open rocks and dug down into the soil.

 Complete the summary below.

Recently, thanks to orbiters, landers and rovers, we have learned many new facts about Mars. These include the news that snow falls on Mars, although it

1 ... *vaporises* ... on its way down.

Explanation: The highlighted words in the text show where you can find the answer. The word you need for **1** is a verb in the third person singular present simple and the 'it' refers back in the summary to 'snow'. Note the different words in the summary, e.g. 'on its way down' rather than 'before it reaches the ground' – and that the order of the information in the paragraph has been changed.

The missing words in the summary may not be in the order they appear in the text.

General tips for **Reading**

1 If you are unable to answer the question, move on to the next question rather than spend too much time on it.

2 Remember to read all the instructions carefully.

3 Note that the questions in most tasks follow the order of the information in the text, but in some they don't (e.g. summary/note/table completion).

4 Where you have to write words, check spelling carefully (the word(s) will always be in the text) and make sure you do not write more than the maximum word limit for that question type.

5 You could save time by writing your answers directly onto the answer sheet, rather than transferring them at the end of the test.

6 Leave time to check your answers at the end of the test.

 NOW YOU TRY! You will find a complete Reading test to try on the CD-ROM.

When you have finished, you can see your scores, check and print your answers.

University of Cambridge ESOL Examinations

The IELTS Writing test

What's in the General Training Writing test?

Task 1 You have to respond to a given problem by writing a letter which requests information or explains a situation.

You have to write at least 150 words.

Task 2 You have to write a short essay in response to a topic which is presented as a point of view, an argument or a problem.

You have to write at least 250 words.

☑ Task 2 contributes twice as much as Task 1 to the Writing score.

🕘 **1 hour**
(about 20 minutes for Task 1 and 40 minutes for Task 2)

Writing: Task 1

 TIP: Make sure you deal with all the points that you need to cover in your answer.

Example

Here is an example of a Task 1 question. The instructions tell you who to write to and why you are writing.

 You have had a problem with your next-door neighbour. You have not been able to speak to the neighbour about this.

Write a **letter** to this neighbour. In your letter:

- explain the problem
- suggest a solution
- say what action you will take if the situation does not improve.

Here is an example of a student answer which covers each of the main points.

Introduction:

I am writing to you because of the noise late at night coming from your flat. I have tried to contact you by telephone on a number of occasions, but there was no response. I'm afraid that the noise has caused considerable disturbance to me and my family.

Explain the problem:

Every night the sound of musical instruments can be heard clearly through the walls of my flat and this goes on until the early hours of the morning, which prevents anyone in my family from getting a good night's sleep.

Suggest a solution:

I would like to suggest that you invest in
soundproofing for your walls to prevent the noise
coming through and disturbing your neighbours.
Furthermore, I would appreciate it if you could stop
playing musical instruments by midnight at the latest.

Say what action you will take if the situation does not improve:

I very much hope that you will do something about
this or I regret that I will have to inform the local
authorities about the disturbance being caused.

Write in a polite style even if you are
complaining about something.

Writing: Task 2

 TIP: Make sure you follow the instructions and answer all parts of the question appropriately.

Example

Here is an example of a Task 2 question. You have to write at least 250 words about the following topic.

 In many countries people are eating more and more unhealthy food and taking less exercise.

What do you think are the causes of this problem and what can be done about it?

Here are some example parts of what a student wrote to answer this question.

> ### Causes of the problem
> One of the reasons why the number of people eating food that is less nutritious is increasing is that there is so much fast food available nowadays. This type of food is often very affordable and as a result of price and availability more and more of it is consumed.
>
> ### What can be done about it?
> One possible solution to the problem could be to improve the amount of education about food and health given to schoolchildren. This would help them to make more informed choices about what they eat both as children and as adults.

Explanation: This question asks you to talk about **two** things – the causes of a problem and what can be done about it.

Writing: Task 2

 TIP: You should include examples from your own experience, but make sure that they are relevant to the question and not too personal.

Example

Here is an example of a Task 2 question.

 In many countries people are eating more and more unhealthy food and taking less exercise.

What do you think are the causes of this problem and what can be done about it?

Here are parts of answers written by students.

Student A

> My friends always eat at fast food burger bars and they are getting really fat and unhealthy. I always tell them they should eat more healthy food.

Student B

> Many people where I live eat at fast food outlets and as a result of the lack of good healthy food their health is suffering and they are gaining weight.

Explanation: The first example is too personal and not totally relevant to the question. The second example is a more relevant and less personal way of saying something similar.

General tips for **Writing**

1 Before you start writing, plan what you are going to say. Make sure you are going to answer the question, rather than writing something irrelevant or too general – there isn't time for this in the test.

2 Use a range of vocabulary and structures to demonstrate your knowledge of English.

3 Make sure you use a range of tenses accurately and appropriately to answer the question.

4 Check that you have written enough words. When you practise writing, count the number of words you have written so you have a good idea of what 150 or 250 words look like in your handwriting.

5 In Task 1, check you have included all the information you have been asked to write about.

6 In Task 2, make sure you support what you say with appropriate examples.

 NOW YOU TRY! You will find a complete Writing test to try on the CD-ROM.

When you have finished you can compare your answers against the sample answers.

The IELTS Speaking test

What's in the Speaking test?

Part 1 Ⓠ You answer general questions about yourself, your home/family, your job/studies, your interests and a range of familiar topic areas.

Part 2 Ⓠ The examiner gives you a card which asks you to talk about a particular topic and which includes points that you can cover in your talk. You are given one minute to prepare: you can make some notes if you wish. You talk for up to 2 minutes, after which the examiner may then ask one or two questions on the same topic.

Part 3 Ⓠ The examiner asks you further questions which are connected to the topic of Part 2. These questions give you an opportunity to discuss more abstract issues and ideas.

  11–14 minutes
The whole Speaking test is recorded.

Speaking: Part 1

 TIP: Explain your answers by giving reasons for what you say.

Example

Here are some examples of answers to questions on familiar topics.

EXAMINER:	What's your favourite place to relax in your home?
CANDIDATE:	Oh, definitely the balcony because if it's warm weather I really enjoy sitting out there in the open air reading a book or just watching the world go by.

EXAMINER:	Have you ever cooked a meal for a lot of people?
CANDIDATE:	Yes, lots of times. I love cooking for other people. Recently I made a big dinner for some of my friends from college. Actually, it was all traditional food from my country and everyone said they really liked it.

EXAMINER:	Are you planning to see any films in the near future?
CANDIDATE:	Well, I've heard there's a new Will Smith film coming out so I'd really like to see that. I've seen most of his films already. In fact, I go to the cinema quite a lot.

Explanation: The highlighted words show how you can organise your responses and explain your answers.

Speaking: Part 1

 TIP: Be prepared to answer questions using different tenses and verb forms.

Example

Here are some questions and typical answers. These answers cover a range of time frames.

EXAMINER: **How long have you had this job?**

CANDIDATE: Well, I started working there about eight months ago and I'm hoping to continue with it until I go back to my country because I'm really enjoying the work I'm doing.

EXAMINER: **Are you going to travel anywhere later this year?**

CANDIDATE: Yes, I'm planning to visit Greece later in the summer with a couple of my friends. That's because we want to go and see the famous ancient ruins and relax on the beach for some of the time, of course.

Explanation: Look at the highlighted examples to see how a range of forms are used to talk about the past, present and future.

Speaking: Part 3

 TIP: Give your opinion and develop your ideas by offering examples of what you mean.

Example

Here is an example of the kind of question you may get in Part 3 and part of a candidate answer.

> **EXAMINER:** **What qualities do you think are important in a good friend?**
>
> CANDIDATE: Well, as far as I'm concerned, some of the most important things are trust and being supportive. What I mean is that a good friend should be someone that you can always depend on and turn to if you need them and you would do the same for them. For example, if you lost your job, a good friend might help you out by lending you money. They would know that you would pay it back and that you'd do the same thing if they were in the same situation.

Explanation: The highlighted words show good examples of developing ideas by adding details and examples.

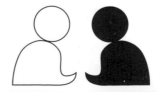

Here are some useful phrases for giving your opinion.

Giving your opinion

In my view . . .

As far as I'm concerned . . .

That's a difficult question . . .

To be honest, I think . . .

Generally speaking, I'd say . . .

I'm not sure what I think about that . . .

I have mixed views on that . . .

Well, on the whole, I tend to agree that . . .

My view is that . . .

It seems to me that . . .

If you ask me . . .

Always give an opinion! It doesn't matter what your opinion is – you are being assessed on your language, not your ideas. The examiner wants to hear how wide your range of language is.

7. Double click the *Top Tips for IELTS* folder to view its contents.
8. Then double click the *Top Tips for IELTS (General Training)* file to launch *Top Tips for IELTS (General Training)*.
9. NOTE: To easily open *Top Tips for IELTS (General Training)*, you can drag it to the dock.
10. To uninstall the application move the *Top Tips for IELTS (General Training)* folder from the Applications folder to the Trash.

System requirements

For PC
Essential:	Windows 2000, XP or Vista, CD Drive and audio capabilities
Recommended:	400 MHz processor or faster, with 256mb of RAM or more

For Mac
Essential:	Mac OS X, version 10.4 or higher
Recommended:	400 MHz G3 processor or faster, with 256mb of RAM or more